Effective Job Hunting

How to organise your job search, write a great Curriculum Vitae (CV) or Résumé, and prepare for interview

By
David Dand

Table of Contents

Introduction 1
Part 1 2
Lessons learnt from my personal experience 2
   A bad start 2
   A Prospecting CV, get them to find you a job; FAST! 16
   Curriculum Vitae: Mitzel Dand 19
Part 2 23
Job search, starting from scratch 23
   Preparation 25
      1. Decide what you want 25
      2. Write your basic CV/Résumé 31
      3. Set up and review your social media 46
      4. General interview preparation 48
      5. Write your pitch 56
      6. Prepare stationary 58
   Organising your job search 59
      1. Reality check 59
      2. Job search strategies: 61
      3. Admin and spreadsheets 65
      4. Cover letters 66
   Landing the job (closing the deal) 68
      1. Dress for success 68
      2. Specific interview preparation - research 69
      3. Second interviews 72
      4. Thank you notes/letters 75

 5. First day on the job 77
Shortened links mentioned in the text **79**
Other reading **81**
 Getting personal help – Skype consultation 81

Introduction

Welcome and thank you for buying my course. Your contribution is much appreciated. In return, you will find here, all that you need to organise and prepare yourself for the task of quickly finding work or, for the more discerning, 'the job of your dreams!'

I have lived long enough to acquire sufficient life experience to know that a well-written CV can be a gold mine. Unfortunately for me, I was always better at getting jobs than keeping them. I have a restless nature and got bored quickly in most of my jobs, so finding a new job was something I did a lot of. It turned out that I am someone who likes to work for himself. Indeed, my CV writing experience became even more valuable as I entered the software contracting world as a freelancer.

If you want to 'cut to the chase,' go directly to Part 2. Part 1 is about me and my experiences and the lessons I have learnt, which I would like to offer you. In Part 2, I use my personal experience to explain some concepts or to make a point, but it is intended to be a practical handbook about going through all the logical steps to find a good job that is suited to you and is the real meat of this publication.

Part 1

Lessons learnt from my personal experience

A bad start

I want offer you the lessons learnt from my personal experience as I tell you a little about my working life: My father decided to give me an excellent education, so from the age of seven, I was packed off to boarding school. My schooling was the best, but I hated every minute. For me, it felt like a life sentence in prison! When I turned sixteen, I walked out of school refusing to take any exams to the horror of my parents and the headmaster. There was nothing they could do or say to get me back. I wanted to be a motor mechanic and that was that!

To my credit, I worked hard to find a job as a trainee. I literally got on my bike and visited every garage in the area. I had no success initially, so my first job was cleaning toilets at a camp site. After that, a few weeks summer job working at a biology research centre that I really enjoyed. Then I had a series of little jobs, including: working on a farm, in a fish and chip shop, and some youth employment work doing painting and decorating. On one occasion, I worked as a grave digger.

At the age of seventeen, I finally got employment in a garage, working on car bodies. The pay was really bad, and I was treated like a slave. However, after six months, this valuable experience brought me the opportunity to work at another garage. It was a one-man band, and I became his helper. He was a nice guy, but he was broke and didn't pay me regularly. Like my previous job, this experience gave me a leg up, and I finally got a job in a 'real garage' where I worked until the end of my apprenticeship and gained the qualification that I had coveted so much during my mid-teens. I had finally made it. The only problem was, I had come to hate working on cars; a complete turnaround from what had, at first, been pleasurable work. So, after five years of training, I quit and have never done this kind of work since. I will say that the knowledge I acquired during this period of my life has often been useful, no one can 'bullshit me' when I take my car to be repaired at least.

You may be wondering why I am telling you all this. Well, it is because I want you to know me a little better. Firstly, because this was my time at the 'university of life,' and I hope my experience will give you food for thought as I explain how I fumbled through my existence and offer you an analysis, as hard-earned wisdom, that you can use on your journey along the path of your working life.

Secondly, and shamefully commercial, because as you work through this training, I want to offer you a personalised online service to check your CV and give you live interview practice on a 'one-on-one' basis. This is just a fancy way of saying that, for a fee, you can talk to me on Skype, and I will give you feedback and advice on your CV, as well as give you a job interview from hell where you can safely test your responses to likely questions or uncover questions that you may, as yet, not have thought of. See the last page for more details.

Finally, despite getting off to what I consider to be a bad start, I want to show you how I was able to turn all of this dubious work history into CVs that were impressive enough to get employers to commit to paying me a salary. So, on with my story...

Even though at the time, I felt very negative about my work history, there was good to be found within. I had stuck out my apprenticeship to the end, and I hadn't needed to live off the state as many of my friends had needed to do at the time. There was a serious lack of work in those days. I was twenty-one, and after recently discovering the pleasures of skydiving, I decided to become a fighter pilot. Yes, I was very serious! There was, of course, a problem. I had left school without taking my 'O' level exams and I needed five 'O' levels, including English and Maths just to be considered. I spent the next nine months, now highly motivated, studying to pass them and I succeeded!

Armed with my exam passes, I went to the RAF (Royal Air Force) recruiting office and applied for a job as a fighter pilot. 'I crashed and burned' at Biggin Hill. (I should tell you that all this was before Top Gun was released.) I had no idea what to expect to find on the aptitude tests and failed miserably and was told never to return. However, I scored a maximum possible score on the mechanical aptitude tests and was offered a position in the RAF as a trainee aeroplane mechanic. Rightly or wrongly, I turned them down flat as I didn't want to be fixing up a jet for someone else to fly! At the time, I was an 'adrenalin junkie,' it scares me now to think how I used to ride my motorbike. It was only my lightning fast reactions that kept me alive. Needless to say, anything other than travelling at 'Mach two with my hair on fire' wasn't going to keep me happy or so I thought at the time.

Over the following ten years, I got married and had kids, I started a riding school, did coal delivery in the winter months, sold life insurance for a couple of years, sold timeshare for a few months, worked as a warranty coordinator in an agricultural machine factory for a year, sold cleaning chemicals, started a business selling cleaning chemicals, got deep into debt*, got my home repossessed by the bank, got divorced and then, having hit the rock bottom, I left the UK to get a break from creditors chasing me and to take stock of my life. What a mess!

The cause of my debt was not due to my businesses failing, but to a combination of complications with local housing planners and to the super high-interest rates imposed on the nation at the time by Mrs Thatcher's government, which left me with the cost of my home on overdraft and my bank charging me an unauthorised interest rate of 36%.

My mother lived in France; I had lost everything, including my home, so it was convenient to spend time with her. The sudden loss of my father taught me that you shouldn't take the existence of loved ones for granted, so I decided to stay on to make up for time lost while I was away at boarding school. Now that she has passed on, I am very glad I made this decision.

I was in my early thirties, I had no money, and I didn't want to live off Mum, so I started to think about how to make a living again. Where she lived was very isolated, and there were no opportunities to be had locally. Even if I could find work, I didn't speak French, so my options were severely limited. I was not really thinking about a career at this time, rather just money that could be reasonably sustainable. My mum lived near a motorway, and at the time, there were a lot of UK-registered trucks going up and down from England to Spain. In those days, the UK dominated European transport. It occurred to me that there was an opportunity here, but I neither had experience or a licence to drive a truck (these were the biggest on the road).

Creativity has got me what I needed; I did some hitch-hiking! In fact, it was Neil, the first driver who gave me a lift who offered to give me some training. My mechanical knowledge served as a bonus as drivers needed to be able to handle problems abroad and a deal was struck. Twelve months later I was driving my own truck and popping in to see Mum on the way past to Spain. Neil used to go to Spain and back to the UK about once every week to ten days, so I would normally just drive the truck in Southern France and Spain, leaving me a few days while he went to the UK to reload. I used this time to study for a new career with computers.

One day, on a visit to see my children, I had been looking in a bookshop for inspiration and came across a book called "Zen and the art of making a living." I bought the book and studied it in depth. I would like to thank Laurence G. Boldt for his magnificent work that still inspires me today. With his help, I did indeed succeed in carving out a new career in IT (Information Technology).

I didn't have a CV that was suitable for a career in IT, so I set about making one. The year 1995 was a year of opportunity for me. I had been interested in computers since my late teens when the very first BBC computers started to appear in shops. In about 1987, during my stint with the life insurance company, I was introduced to the first generation of modern computers, the Intel 8086 family to be precise. In 1988, I got my IBM - see the picture. There was no Windows then, just MS DOS, but this machine inspired me to learn IBM Basic. By 1990, I had got a modem and was able to get data from BT Prestel service and load business names into my database.

I connected to the Internet in 1991 via CompuServe, but was put off by the price. Then I took a 4-year break while I did my truck driving in Spain. In 1995, I was driving my truck, listening to the radio when I heard someone raving about the World Wide Web. I remember thinking to myself, '...that must be that CompuServe thing that I was doing all those years ago.' When I got home, I dug my old computer out of the attic, fixed the hard drive that had caused me to stop computing in the first place and connected to the Internet (CompuServe very kindly sent me their software on 5 1/4" Floppy Disks). I realised that my equipment was well out of date, so I just went out and bought a new computer with this weird new operating system, Windows 95.

In 1991, I only knew a handful of people with computers. Few people had anticipated the sudden mass take-up of computers, which happened during the early 1990s, but by 1995, I had seen the light. I was going to have a career in Internet programming, so I started a company in France and set about learning my new craft with the Open University. After 5 years of doing websites for people, I closed the company and went to London and got myself work as a Perl Programmer in London. It is never too late to build a new career.

Today, I have had many years of experience, and I am qualified to postgraduate level (Liverpool University 2003). In the end, I became the 'real deal.' If you are struggling to get your working life together, you need to re-write your CV like I did. Creating a 'dot com' start up, in the beginning, was really bluffing, but I was able to turn the vision into reality by 'acting out' my plan inspired by "Zen and the art of making a living." In a nutshell, you make your plan, and one day you get out of bed and say to yourself, 'As from today, I am a...' In my case, I said; 'As of today, I am a Web Programmer' and, as I mentioned, in due course, it came about as I acted out my plan.

Some lessons I have learnt that can help you get work and stay in a job

We all have strengths and weaknesses. We have all achieved, and we have all done things that we regret. People's lives are very diverse, both in their backgrounds, their desires, and their experience in life. I cannot, therefore, give you a standard CV template that will work for everyone in every situation. If that was the case, the person who changed the template would get the job. The trick is to identify your achievements, even if you don't think they are a big deal, often others do. Recognise your weaker points and start to do something about them with positive action. The general rule is, excel with your strengths, but don't allow yourself to be let down by your weak points; work on them till you achieve an acceptable level or competence. You must think positively and present yourself with confidence, even if you don't feel that way on the inside. It is not a lie to try to project confidence, you are acting, and we all do that in life even if we don't know it. If you play the role long enough, you 'become the role.'

Here is a list of the ten top working values employers look for in individuals:

1. **Strong Work Ethic:** willingness to work hard and work smart.
2. **Dependability and Responsibility:** get to work on time and be where you are supposed to be - be responsible for your actions and behaviour. Keep your supervisor informed of where you are on all projects, be dependable.
3. **Possessing a Positive Attitude:** take the initiative and have the motivation to get jobs done in a reasonable period of time. A positive attitude inspires others.
4. **Work Adaptability:** be able to complete diverse tasks in an ever changing workplace.
5. **Adaptable Personality:** means adapting to the personality and work habits of co-workers and supervisors.

6. **Honesty and Integrity:** your boss and colleagues can trust what you say and what you do.
7. **Self-Motivated:** be motivated to grow and learn.
8. **Strong Self-Confidence:** self-confidence has been recognized as the key ingredient between someone who is successful and someone who is not.
9. **Professional Behaviour:** includes learning every aspect of a job and doing it to the best of one's ability. Professionals look, speak, and dress accordingly to maintain an image of someone who takes pride in their behaviour and appearance.
10. **Loyalty:** be trustworthy and exhibit loyalty to the company.

Aspire to these traits and they will serve you well. Also, remember that every job you do in life is important, even if you think it is below you. You are acquiring experience and knowledge, but not only that, if you do the job to the best of your ability, you will start to enjoy the work more. When the day comes for you to move on to another job, hopefully, you will also get a good reference and maybe more. Let me tell you a little anecdote from my past experience to illustrate my point.

A few years ago, I was between 'official' jobs. I was making some money from the Internet and doing part-time truck driving work (there was very little driving work as I was living in a national park), none of which gave me a payslip. However, I wanted to bring my wife from the Philippines. In short, to satisfy immigration requirements, I needed an official job with payslips. I applied for the first job I saw; washing up in a busy restaurant. I have worked as a computer programmer in the City of London on financial systems, a job that gave me a lot of respect and had boosted my self-esteem. Naturally, I felt I could do better than washing up, but it solved my immediate problem of the payslips, so I took the job.

It was really hard work, crockery from the dining room, burnt pans and trays from the kitchen kept piling up relentlessly for me to wash. The restaurant was chaotic due to a narrow passage leading to the kitchen where all the waitresses would come scuttling down to pick up the food. Part of my job was to put the clean plates on shelves in this passage and take the glasses and cutlery to the dining area also via the same passage. This resulted in many collisions with the speeding front of house staff who were very unhappy about me blocking their way!

I have a system builder personality, so I could see the current system was inefficient. Hence, I decided to devise a new system. I spoke to the boss and explained the problem and that it could be solved by several plastic trays and some cooperation with the front of house staff. At first, the waitresses thought I was shirking my duties because they had to take the trays of glasses to the dining room and drop off the plates in the passage. I explained to them that half the time, they were making the journey with empty hands, so it should be no big deal to grab a tray on the way past, and besides, I would no longer be blocking their way. They were still reluctant, but after a couple of days, everyone had agreed that everything was now running much more smoothly and I was able to focus on clearing the backlog of kitchen pots.

I took pleasure in optimising every little aspect of the process until I got to a point when as soon as a dirty item was put for me to wash, it would immediately be dealt with. Suddenly, I realised I was having fun. The kitchen staff was a crew of twenty-somethings, and we used to have a good laugh while getting things done. One day, the head chef announced that I was the best 'washer upper,' they had ever had working there. His compliment made me feel proud.

The benefits didn't stop there; I was also making money on the Internet giving Skype English lessons in the mornings before going to work, so I was making quite a bit of money, putting it all together. It turned out that the payslips weren't enough for the immigration authorities. It was necessary to rent another, bigger, flat within a fifteen-day deadline in order to respond, by appeal, to the refusal of my wife's immigration application. I desperately searched for properties to rent for several days, but to no avail. I didn't know what to do to resolve the situation; disaster was looming!

I mentioned my problem to one of the ladies who told me that Tony, the boss, had a flat upstairs. I spoke to Tony, and thanks to my good work ethic, he gave me the flat to rent and by doing so, saved the day. My immigration appeal succeeded due to having the payslips and the flat. Today, 8 years later, my wife is a British citizen and we are still happily married. All thanks to 'the dead end' washing up job. The moral of this little tale is to take all your jobs seriously, even those that don't interest you much. Do the work well, and it may bring you unexpected rewards. Later on, I revamped the restaurant's website and added this to my CV, which helped secure my next IT job.

Getting a job is just sales and marketing!

If you are going to sell a product, any product, then there are certain steps you will have to take. In all cases, step 1 is to, somehow, tell your potential customers about it. If you don't, nothing happens - no sales, nobody even knows that you are trying to sell something! It follows then that you have to get your message out in some form or the other.

When I was selling life insurance, the basic process was this. Get the phone book (pre-Internet days), and phone 40 people and ask them if they want to buy your product, or rather, make an appointment to talk to them about the products at this stage. Some people are really tough and can do this day-in-day-out, but I can tell you it sucks! I used to get sick of the sound of my own voice repeating the same lines over and over again. Most people will give you some kind of excuse not to see you, very often they would say, 'Oh, err.., put something in the post.' Then you think, I hate making these calls, so I will post my brochure and then call them in a few days. What you find is, they are now forewarned to say 'no' and have a better excuse ready like, 'Yes, I read your brochure, sorry, but I am not interested; goodbye!'

Everyone who works in sales knows to a certain extent that it's a numbers game. After a time, you can review your performance and see that you are closing, say for example, one in twenty-five people you talk to or from one in ten first appointments. Actually, the averages become very consistent over time, and you can use this as motivation. I used to make a chart that looked a bit like those pool knockout competition score charts. On the left, there was a column containing the names and numbers of all the people I intended to call, and the next column was the names of those who made an appointment (the fact finds interview). The third column was the names that went to the second/third appointment (product presentation) and finally on the right were the names of the people who bought a product together with the commission earned. The average was about £200 (GBP) for every twenty people that I spoke to. The snag was that it has been often about three months before the results could be seen. However, if you divide the earnings by the number of calls made, you would normally have a figure of about £4.00 (GBP) per call. Then when someone told me where I could stick my product, I could reply or think, 'Thank you, you just earned me £4.00!'

When I used to send out brochures about life insurance products and put off making the calls for a few more days, occasionally, maybe about one in a thousand would call me and ask me to come to visit them. A sale wasn't guaranteed, but it felt good to be genuinely invited. In the end, I found that walking into shops or small businesses and striking up a conversation worked for me.

People were usually busy, but their body language would 'tell' as I briefly spoke about the products and I could detect both from what they said and did as to their level of interest. I didn't push them for appointments, but just noted their names and phone numbers. Inevitably, when I called them a few days later, they were 'warm' and friendly and would nearly always make an appointment for me to see them. Other benefits were exercise and a feeling that I had done a good day's work. I tracked the numbers by handing out business cards, and when I had no cards left, I had reached my target for the day.

A note on rejection

When job hunting, the product is you, and your brochure is your CV. You are going to be rejected, don't take it personally. It may be that you were not 'good enough' for them in some way or they failed to spot your potential, but you must be tough and tell yourself that it was their loss. Don't dwell on it; sales is 95% failure. Just remember that every failure you get is one step nearer to success; you will get there in the end! The RAF told me that my reactions were slow, but the truth is that I wasn't used to operating the gadget they gave me in the test. If I accidentally knock a glass of a table, nine times out of ten, I will catch it before it hits the ground. As for thinking under pressure, one day back in the early 1980's while skydiving, my parachute failed, so I cut it away, as one should, then after several seconds, it became clear that my reserve parachute hadn't opened. I had had a total malfunction, and I was falling to my death!

An old 'coffee stained' photo from the 1980s featuring the

offending parachute system

However, I collected my thoughts and performed the 'funky chicken' manoeuvre. My actions saved my life with just a few hundred feet to spare! The RAF lost a good pilot the day they told me to go home. Some years later, I took flying lessons and was cleared to fly solo after 8 hours, and the RAF says that any of their pilots worth their salt clear to fly solo in the minimum time of 8 hours. Their loss! But maybe they got it right because I just wanted to fly fast jets, I would have really not wanted to drop bombs on people! Clearly, it wasn't my destiny. If you fail to get a job, put it behind you and get on with looking for another opportunity. Remember, you learn more from failure than success, or so they say.

A Prospecting CV, get them to find you a job; FAST!

If you even need a CV, it must have a purpose and be aimed at an idea; a specific job role or even focused on a job at one particular company in certain cases. (If you find a particular position important enough to merit it.)

One option, if you need money fast, is to create what I call a 'prospecting CV.' I drafted a general CV like this, many years ago, that was not aimed at a specific job, but its purpose was to offer the recipient the opportunity to find a job that suited me. It worked and not just on one occasion. I used the idea twice and got good jobs as a result. I am referring to the time when I worked as a warranty coordinator in an agricultural machine factory and then later when I found work selling cleaning chemicals. I would have never normally applied for either of these jobs. The recipients looked at my experience and motivation and called me. Indeed, during one of these campaigns, I recall someone from a local newspaper phoned to tell me that he was very sorry that there were no openings in his organisation at that time, but he had greatly appreciated my CV and would have very much liked to have hired me. He also pointed out some small errors I had made in my CV; he was a newspaper editor and was very in tune with proofreading. I should tell you that I did this in pre-Internet days (hard to imagine now). From the Town Hall, I obtained 500 mailing labels of local business over a certain size and sent them all by regular post on the same day. A few days later, I was choosing between job offers. I had to make some hard choices, but it was a good position to be in. The next section is about finding the job you love, but if you are just prepared to take what comes for now and are prepared to roll up your sleeves and get your hands dirty, then this method may be for you.

Here is an example of a prospecting CV that I did for my wife using Google Drive docs and exported for printing in pdf format. Actually, it was more like a colour brochure, crossed with an application form. The method she used was simply to print out copies and hand them out in the village to possible employers. She had resigned all her jobs the year before, but wanted to return to work for the summer coming up. I had already collected many application forms from local businesses that were hiring people for positions such as cleaners, shop assistants, restaurant workers, and assembled the information they were asking for. This is why I have included some information that you would not normally put on a CV. My wife has a bubbly personality, but not many academic skills (although she does speak three languages fluently). It was very likely that the sort of people who would hire her would be looking for employees to do 'customer facing roles,' so for this reason, I used lots of photos and colour to show off her smart appearance. It is eye catching, and it sends some subliminal messages, i.e., it is saying she is creative, has initiative and she is a hard worker. After all, she has made an effort to call in person. These are positives not even mentioned in the CV.

The CV is longer than normal, covering three pages (sides) of A4 including a detailed work history that was relegated to the third page. All the important stuff, though, is at the top of the first page in a profile that is easily digestible in a glance of a few seconds. If the readers were interested, they would have read on. All the information needed to make a hiring decision is there as is all the necessary information to make an informed decision to discard the CV. We don't want to waste people's time. She had a job offer by the end of the first day and started the following day.

One little abnormal addition to look out for is the 3rd party testimonial from me about my wife. In sales, testimonials are very strong as you will probably know. Here, my testimonial is used to reinforce her best qualities (I do not recommend this format as a template - see the template structure in part 2). When the day comes for her to use her CV again, I plan to make some changes.

However, it was suitably impressive, and it got the message out and, at the end of the day, that is what was important.

Curriculum Vitae: Mitzel Dand

Introduction:

Hello, my name is Mitzel. I am a British Citizen and have lived in Windermere. I've had six years of experience with Lakeland Limited as a cleaner. I also cleaned in the Santander Bank in Windermere for 3 years. Last August 2015, I moved with my husband to France to help him renovate a property that he recently acquired. As I don't speak French, I am not able to work in France. I have, therefore, decided to come to Windermere to work the summer season. Lakeland Limited offered to re-engage me for 20 hours per week, which will include Monday to Friday evenings from 5 pm to 9 pm. I am currently looking for work to fill my time outside of these hours. Thank you for reading my CV.

Personal Information:
Surname: Dand
Forenames: Mitzel Gonzales
Preferred Name: Mrs Mitzel Dand
Next of Kin: David Dand
Address: ████████, ████████, France
Telephone **Mob:** **Telephone home:**
████████
Email address: ████████

Education:

From	To	School	Qualifications obtained
1981	1988	Gusa Elementary School	Graduated

| 1988 | 1992 | Cathedral High School | Graduated |
| 1992 | Nov 1993 | Liceo de Cagyan University | First year only. |

Hobbies and Interests:
I like cooking and cake baking, and using the Internet to communicate with my friends. I am also interested in clothing and fashion.

Employment History:
Please see next sheet.

Languages Spoken:
Visayan, Tagalog, and English

Right to work and ethnic origin:
I am a British Citizen, and I have the right to work in the UK.
My British passport number is: ■■■■■■ and my National Insurance Number is: ■■■■■■.
My ethnic origin is Filipino.

Medical History:
I have no medical problems, and I am not taking any medication or drugs of any kind.

Criminal convictions:
I have no criminal convictions or any cases pending. I have a recent CRB Certificate disclosure number ■■■■■■ dated 12/November 2010. Police record of convictions, etc. NONE RECORDED

Referees:

Relationship: former employer and friend

Relationship: manager and friend at Lakeland LTD

* Please do not contact referees unless a position is offered to me.

Mitzel is incredibly hardworking and shows great initiative. Since late 2010, she has held down 3 and sometimes 4 part time jobs to make up a full-time wage and additionally, has made extra money selling items on eBay that she has sourced locally and over the Internet. Everyone loves her outgoing personality which together with her natural empathy makes her ideally suited for customer facing roles.

More English than the English. Mitzel loves England and live in the UK. Mitzel is a happy person, and her smile and enthusiasm are infectious.

Ever since I have known Mitzel, she has impressed her colleagues and me with her honesty and her affectionate nature. That's why I married her, and that's why you won't regret employing her. (A biased, but sincere mini reference by David Dand.)

The employment history page was done on a Google Drive spreadsheet and exported in landscape pdf format to allow for the width of the page. It printed neatly onto one sheet of A4 paper. The column titles were as follows:

From
To
Job title and brief description of role
Employer's full name, address, and postcode
Telephone number
Hours worked
Reason for leaving
Final wage

Part 2

Job search, starting from scratch

Going for your dream job

Before suggesting to you how you should go about finding your dream job, I want to mention my sister. She was in her early twenties and had had a few jobs, but hadn't found anything that worked for her. She went to an interview for a job as an office junior with a small local engineering company and was offered a job. She told me later that she had accepted because she liked the feel of the place and the general friendly atmosphere. I am very proud of my sister because the company grew and she worked consistently, as well as studied at nights at the Open University to pass accounting and business studies exams without complaint for many years. In due course, the company was bought out by a big multinational engineering company. Today, she still works there, but for the last 10 years, she has been a director and the UK CEO. She became the boss and heads up a team of several hundred employees. Patience and loyalty can pay off.

Whether you have just finished university or you've been made redundant, the day comes when you need to do a job search. If you have studied hard and got good qualifications, you may not relish the idea of rushing out and grabbing any work you can get your hands on. You have put in the study time, and now you want the pay-off! Here are the steps to take. This is the overview, and I will go through each of the steps in detail over the next pages:

Preparation

1. Decide what you want
2. Write your base résumé
3. Set up and review your social media
4. General interview preparation
5. Write your pitch
6. Prepare stationary

Organising your job search

1. Reality check
2. Job search strategies
3. Admin and spreadsheets
4. Cover letters

Landing the job (closing the deal)

1. Dress for success
2. Specific Interview prep - research the company
3. Second interviews
4. Thank you notes/letters
5. First day on the job

Preparation

1. Decide what you want

If you are already focused and decided, you may want to skip this section. However, the tests are quite fun, and it doesn't do any harm to reflect on your current situation from time to time. This section is aimed at people setting off in their work life and individuals who later, down the line, start to feel confused as I did in my early thirties. Who am I? And what in the world am I doing here? Are the big questions to ask yourself according to Laurence G. Boldt, author of "Zen and the art of making a living." A heavy read, but well worth the effort if you are struggling to find what you want to do in life. However, here is a short 3-step formula for those in a hurry.

Step One - Motivation

Try to understand what motivates you, ask yourself these questions:
(There are links to useful free test that may help your thinking)

- What sort of things do I do well? - Test: what are your strengths? (1) *
- What triggers and keeps my interest? – Tip: ask your parents and your close friends
- What kind of personality do I have? - Try this Personality Test (2)
- What values are really important to me? Test to help you find your values (3)
- What experience do I have?

Link shortcuts can be found at the end of the book

In the www.humanmetrics.com test, I came out as an INTJ (4) personality type with some INTP (5) traits. I found the descriptions to be weirdly accurate! The INTJ type is described as the 'Systems Builder,' and I do agree, that is me!

What you did in step one is evaluating who you are and identifying what you are naturally being drawn to. (What in the world am I doing here?) This awareness should help you find the kind of work that you will enjoy doing. You will probably spend most of your life at work (on average, 80,000 hours), so you need to make sure it is what you want to do, something that makes you feel satisfied and something you will, in due course, be able to look back on and be proud of. Laurence G. Boldt, in his book, "Zen and the art of making a living," puts a great emphasis on finding your work purpose based on your personal talents, values, interests, and experience. This, in turn, leads you to your career trajectory. Your career trajectory will always point in the same direction, even though it may be composed of many different jobs. He goes on to say that life is a service to others, if your purpose is to help animals, your career path may lead you to become a veterinary surgeon and then on to becoming a wildlife park ranger. The point being that although the two jobs are both very different, they have in common, service to the welfare of animals. This is your career trajectory. You may want to give this some thought because the reference to career trajectory can emerge in interview questions and often does. Employers pick up on a career trajectory as a kind of 'subliminal' clue to your motivation. If your career trajectory is not satisfying you now, then perhaps this is the time to make changes. Here are some questions to ask yourself to help unveil your purpose:

Where am I now?

1. What do I do? (What are my interests? What do I love doing? What do I do a lot of that I find fulfilling? What subject could I go out and teach today because I am already supremely qualified? What in this world matters to me?)
2. Who do I do it for? (Are they Individuals? Groups of people? Animals? Children? The rain forest?)
3. What do these People/Animals want or need?
4. What benefit do they get from me?

Where do I want to be?

1. What can I do for others that is valuable and how can I make the world a better place?
2. What would I really like to achieve?
3. What can I do to inspire myself?

What you can do right now to help prepare

Think about problems you could help solve. They could be global or in your community or something that affects individuals. This will help you identify the value for your skills and mind set.

Push yourself to do things to inspire yourself, learn new marketable skills in areas that you find interesting, play to your strengths and are valuable to the problems you would like to help solve.

Get around like-minded, successful people who inspire you. You can do this by meeting people in person or online via Ted talks or join groups. Very often, these groups lead you to seminars and real world engagements.

Step Two - What careers will suit you

Try this fun test to help you decide: The Holland Code Career test (6)
Learn about your career choices and the various kinds of work you might do, the qualifications needed, and the salary ranges for different occupations. Make a list of possible careers or kinds of work you might want to do. Also, try to think about any negative drawbacks that may affect you over time to decide if these may be a problem for you. Finding out the negatives could save you years of training in the wrong job! Do you remember that I told you I had trained as a car mechanic only to ditch it all after qualifying and 5 years of training? Why did I start to hate the work? It is kind of important because there are lessons to be learnt about aspects of work that are not immediately obvious.

Actually, I enjoy fixing a seriously broken engine or gearbox. What got me down was what one might describe as the 'peripheries' of the job. Work started at 8 am, and it took me about 45 minutes to get to work, which wasn't too bad. The winter months are quite unpleasant in the north of England; cold, damp, and short days. I remember feeling depressed in the winter months as it would be dark when entering work and dark when leaving work at 5:30 pm. I started to feel that I never saw daylight. Additionally, when work started, I would put a car on 'the lift' and go underneath to do the repairs. The car would often be wet or have snow and salt stuck in various 'crevices' of the car body. This freezing saline solution would drip on my head and neck all the time. The spanners were freezing cold, and injuries to my permanently oil-infused hands were frequent.

The summer was not much better because now, it was the heat that made me sweat and that would mix with the oil and grime. I also hated wearing overalls. I was uncomfortable all the time. Then there was working upside down trying to fix some very awkward thingamajig under the steering wheel. The whole job involved discomfort most of the time, not to mention welding when all the hot metal drips and sparks burn you all over your body! Inevitably, one would be far more likely to be positioned under the area to be welded.

Even that was not the reason why I quit. The garage had a system of handing out apprentices to experienced men in rotation. Once you were allocated to someone, you were stuck with him. I was given to George, I liked George a lot, but he was not the best mechanic in the shop.
The best man by popular consent was Clarky. My friend, John, had been Clarky's apprentice. Clarky got all the best jobs; he was constantly doing rebuilds on Jaguar XJ12 engines and gearboxes, both automatic and manual. Doing work like this, for me, was the best possible training that could be had. John got real value from this and was an outstanding mechanic. However, for me who was stuck on the other side of the workshop, I was only being allowed to do oil changes and services, and was completely missing out. This happened basically because George wasn't trusted to do complex work. I tried to complain as not to hurt George's feelings discreetly, but I was told that union rules forbid the changing of mechanics to work with. In the end, I felt I had been short-changed and deprived of the opportunity for the best training available. Finally, I had noticed that even with Clarky's know-how and after twenty-six years of loyal service to the company, he was barely getting paid more than me and my pay wasn't great. It was a combination of all these factors that turned me away from the profession.

The point here is trying to read between the lines in job ads and trying to anticipate some of the potential negative aspects that may come with the job that might, over the long term, give you regrets. All jobs have negatives, and you must decide if you can live with them. Aspects like strange work hours or lots of travel may appeal at first to a single person, but later, when one gets a family, one usually wants to spend time at home.

Step Three - Make a choice

Decide what your priorities are. After you've worked through steps one and two, you should start to have some ideas about what you want to do. Cross off your list the jobs that won't work financially or have other negative factors you can't live with. Keep in mind that there is no reason why you can't change your mind about your career trajectory later on. You may just find out that the reality is not for you as I did with mechanicing. The real love of my life has been computers and programming, but I am careful to take time out periodically so that I don't kill off my passion.

A note on passion

If after you have gone through this, and you are still sitting around and wondering what to do, then just go get a job, any job that you like the sound of. Be open minded and be prepared to be surprised by your new job. Your interests will more than likely change over the years; mine certainly have. Passion is about giving your attention to what is in front of you, and your interest will follow when you dedicate your mind to the job. You are not obliged to follow your passion; you can let your passion follow what you are doing. If someone wants to hire you, then they are showing you what is valuable to them. Put your heart and soul into the job and see what comes back. You will more than likely gain handy new skills and experience, and earn some cash; being useful will feed your soul. If this is where you are now, think about writing a prospecting CV - see part 1.

2. Write your basic CV/Résumé

The sort of issues you may have to encounter

I have always found writing the work experience part of my CV to be the most complicated. I nearly lost a programming job once because I told some stories about my truck driving experience. I know this because my boss told me some months after I had been working for the company. I had found the job advertised in the local Jobcentre. I called the company and was invited to go for an interview immediately. I arrived and presented my CV, it was the very early days of the World Wide Web, and everyone was desperate for web programmers. I showed them my CV and was offered a job on the spot, and I accepted. I was then invited to join the team later on at a social meeting to get to know the other staff members. It was fun and casual, so I told some of the guys about my experiences driving trucks in Spain and the time I nearly slipped off a cliff during a sudden snow storm. The next day, I was asked to come in and design some web pages for a prospective customer. I did it all without a second thought. A few months later when I had really proven my worth, they told me that after hearing my stories, they doubted that I had had the experience that I had claimed on my CV, but had been more than satisfied with the web pages and scripting I had done for them. I had left my truck driving experience out of my CV because it wasn't relevant to web programming.

One of my biggest personal weaknesses is that I find it very hard to maintain a regular routine. I get bored going to the same place to work every day, and I don't know why. I did well as an agency driver as I switch workplaces a lot, we would often go to the same places, but the fact that it was broken up was enough to keep me happy. Another curious thing about me was that, sometimes, I would be working 2 or 3 jobs at the same time.

When I lived in Liverpool, I worked with trucks at night and did a full-time job in the daytime. My day time job started at 10 and continued to 5:30 pm; and normally at 6 pm, I went to work with the driving agency. I would finish between 2 am to 6 am. I slept on my breaks or while waiting to be tasked. It was quite tough, but I did that for about a year. It was a little odd because my colleagues in the day job did their hours and went home for the night and reappeared the next day after an evening at home, but I may have been to London and back during the night! The result was I could produce 2 CVs without gaps. If I wanted a truck work, I had current experience; and if I wanted IT work, I would also have current experience. If you register with an agency for some kind of work, you only have to work quite rarely, but it does account for your time and gives the impression you have been active during that period even if the agency didn't send you much work. I haven't had any time unemployed in 30 years as I have a number of 'tricks' to earn money. I don't know if it works as well now, but a few years ago, you could get cash in hand by packing parachutes. 30 parachutes packed over the weekend could make £150. Another one of my tricks was giving English lessons by Skype. Having a few tricks up your sleeve is an added security.

Even when your boss tells you that he is really happy with your work and you feel very secure in a job, you never know if someone, perhaps trying to cover their own failures, may successfully stab you in the back and use you as a scapegoat. When you don't see it coming, they can make you look really bad. With technical work, management often doesn't have enough understanding to make knowledge-based decisions and rely on what people say and can, therefore, be 'poisoned' in advance of you having your say. People can be very dishonest when covering their failings; watch out, or you will hear yourself uttering Shakespeare's infamous words of Julius Caesar: 'et tu, Brute!' It is not always work, colleagues, but the company's customers too or indeed a combination of both. Yes, I have the bloodstained T-shirt, and I still have the bad taste in my mouth.

Having some tricks to fall back on can allow you to walk away from a position where you are being abused if you are not dependent on their pay cheque. You can just walk away if you so desire or can resign before you get fired if it comes to that. Most firms will not give you a reference other than confirming that you worked for them between certain dates. So you can truthfully say something like, 'It was a good company, but the daily commute was too far, so I started looking elsewhere,' or the famous politician's cliché, 'I wanted to spend more time with my family' and skip over the real reasons.

General tips for writing your employment section

If you read helpful articles on the Internet, they will tell you to craft your employment history to each job you apply for. Well, I wouldn't disagree that they are no doubt correct, but from a practical point of view, this will really slow down your job search. If you really want one very special job, then surely do this. For me, I found that I have never had much success at getting specific positions that I converted. I have painstakingly crafted and sent impressive CVs, just to get no response at all. Employers treat applicants with contempt, remember, research says that they give your CV 3 to 9 seconds before making a preliminary decision and moving on, so, sadly, the chances are your carefully prepared document will not be appreciated. You are probably better off thinking SPAM! Therefore, I would say to you, craft your work history once really well, maybe twice if you have adopted parallel career paths like myself. After all, your work history is a statement of facts, but 'spun' in a way to attract your employer. I personally cover the last 5 to 10 years of my work experience in detail and chronological order with the most recent job at the top. Beyond that and following the 'Work history' section, you can mention experience in a short 'Relevant experience' summary section.

Whenever I want to do something like spending a couple of months abroad, I find myself questioning how my actions will affect my CV the next time I need to write one. Your CV kind of controls your life; which is a bit sad. I may leave out irrelevant stuff out, but I always write the truth. After all, do they really want to know everything you have done in the last 45 years of your life or that you spent a few weeks doing part time coal delivery on the run up to Christmas for some extra money? Using this convenient potential pretext, you can leave out stuff you don't want to talk about. If, for example, during an interview for an IT job, you decide that it would be an advantage for them to know you have heavy goods driving licence, then, by all means, tell them. If your potential employer runs commercial vehicles, your knowledge of the industry and how it works could be your USP (Unique Selling Point) over other candidates. A lot of people tell lies about their employment history. So if employers start to doubt your integrity, then it is here they will look, so make sure you can't be caught out. You can be fired for telling lies on your CV, so be careful, and I would only recommend that you are truthful.

Gaps in your employment history

If you have gaps in your employment history, it is a potential problem. Employers look for this, 'was he or she in prison over this period or why didn't he or she make an effort to find a job?' they may think to themselves. If you have a gap, make sure you have an answer ready for the interview or preferably have it explained on the CV somewhere. If you were doing voluntary work and were not paid, this should not be included in the 'Employment history' section, but rather in the 'Relevant experience' section, mentioned earlier, and detail it there. Show the dates to account for the gap in your employment history. Now, it is explained on your CV.

More tips about the structure of the employment history

section

For employment history, headings include: the 'Full job title,' 'Employer's full name - address, postcode, phone number,' a brief 'Summary,' and 'Start and finish dates.' You could add 'Achievements' and/or 'Reason for leaving.' You must always be ready to answer the reason for leaving a question about any job in an interview (see how to respond to these types of questions in the interview section).

Do not make your brief 'Summary' into a job description. Rather, prove your value, emphasize your accomplishments, and provide proof of your potential value. Wherever possible, include measurable results of your work, in other words, quote figures where you can. Think Achievement and Results; what types of challenges did you face? What actions did you take to overcome the issues? What were the results of your efforts, and how did your performance benefit the company? Write down a list of your Achievements and Results and implement the most impressive into your résumé. A good method is to write the results before listing your actions and achievements. This allows you to keep the most compelling aspects of your accomplishment up front. For example: I increased the company website traffic by 2.5 million visitors per year with the lead generating software that I designed and installed on the company's web server. A 75% traffic boost was achieved overnight when the software went live. Naturally, the company's revenue would have increased too, so you might mention that as another of your achievements.

Question planting

When you are confident about something you have done, and you can make it sound interesting, you can leave out some aspect that will prompt your interviewer to ask you a question about the subject. You will appear modest while allowing your 'clever' interviewer to uncover a hidden gem and give you the opportunity to brag about your achievement so that your interviewer gets all the gory details! In the example above, if you left the last sentence as 'Naturally, the company's revenue increased too,' after seeing such an impressive increase in traffic, any even vaguely curious interviewer would be sorely tempted to ask how much the revenue increased by. Let's hope it was something really impressive! If you do it right, they always ask. Afterwards, they are totally blown away, you can see it in their eyes, 'we've got to get this guy on board!'

Readability

Use paragraphs and bullets in combination. Write your current position in the present tense and previous jobs in the past tense. For each employer, provide a short paragraph that details your responsibilities. Then make a bulleted list of your top contributions. The bullets will draw attention to your accomplishments. Use a heading like 'Achievements' or 'Important Contributions.'

Putting it all together, here is an example:

Employment History:

Start and finish dates: 10/2013 to present date
Employer's name and contact information: Example.com, Some street, London, WC2A 2BE, Tel: +44 (0)20 7415 9887
Job title: Webmaster and system administrator
Summary: Responsible for the development and maintenance of company's websites and Internet marketing strategy. Manage a three-man development team. Organise team meetings and task team members. Supervise the daily operation of the remote Linux servers.

Achievements:
- Increased the company website traffic by 2.5 million visitors per year with the lead generating software that I designed and installed on the company's web server.
- In 6 months, I organised the development team to totally rewrite and implement the company website using the latest Node.js server push technology.
- Cut the company's dependence on paid advertising by 50%.

Start and finish dates: 05/2011 to 09/2013

Employer's name and contact information: Some other place LTD, Another rd,
Anotherton, AN22 4EL, Tel: +44 (0)5354 415 9887

Job title: Web developer

Summary: Member of 4-man team, wrote computer code as according to tasks given in Perl, C++, JavaScript, HTML, CSS

Achievements:
- Successfully completed 9 separate projects using combinations of the above-mentioned technologies.
- Acquired a good knowledge of Agile Methodology and software testing.

Reason for leaving: Wanted to obtain a management role.

NB. Be careful not to overuse phrases like 'responsible for' and 'duties include,' etc.

Targeting a specific job

If you then want to tweak your employment history to target a particular job, you can emphasise items relevant to the job role you are applying for. Personally, I do that in my 'Key skills' section at the beginning of the document.

When I worked for CMG Admiral in London (now Logica), I was hired as an IT consultant. Our first task was to write a CV describing our skills that could be used to sell us to their clients. We didn't present our CVs directly; that was the job of the account managers. We were the product for sale, so we had to write our CVs in the third person. This meant rather than write,' I worked at Some Company LTD,' we had to write 'David worked at Some Company LTD' or 'He worked at Some Company LTD.' The lady consultants would obviously use 'She.' If someone else is presenting your CV, then you might consider doing this.

A relevant experience section

To keep your CV compact, you may decide to stop your employment history description after going back, perhaps 6 years. You might want to mention relevant work experience done outside of this period or if you have gaps in your CV, where you have done voluntary work or done some home study that you don't want to add to your education section. You can put all this in the 'Relevant experience' section underneath your employment history. Use a similar style to the employment history, giving start and finish dates, and the same titles where appropriate or invent new titles when not appropriate. In all cases, you can finish with your bullet pointed achievements as with your employment history. For example:

Start and finish dates: 01/2011 to 04/2011
Home Internet study during a period of unemployment:
Used this time to add to my IT skill set by researching and improving my knowledge of and skills with SQL. I also installed the Linux (Ubuntu) on my home computer and experimented with MySQL and PostgreSQL.
Achievements:
- I obtained a good knowledge of 2 popular open source database systems that subsequently helped me secure my

next job.

Being unemployed is not a disgrace as it once used to be. We have all been there at some time or other. The point is to show that you have used your time for something constructive to aid your career prospects.

The education section:

List your qualifications in order of the most recent or most relevant first. Give details on the title of your qualification and where you studied, the grade you were awarded, and the date you achieved it. You should also give the start and finish dates of the period when you studied. If you have a Ph.D., give the full title of the Ph.D. and the names of your supervisors. Should you include qualifications with no relevance to the job? This is your decision; if you have spent a long period of study, then this says a lot about you. You did the work, and you are intelligent enough to do it. You account for your time and, of course, it is an achievement. You need to make a decision based on your thoughts about the job you are applying for. However, at this stage, if you are following this course, we are working on a base for your résumé. So I suggest you lay it all out at this stage, find all the information you need. If you feel you need to cross something off, it is easily done when preparing for a specific job. You can include qualifications for which you are currently working on as long as you make it clear that you have not finished them yet.

You have now completed the hardest part of the CV; dug back into the past and found out all the dates you worked and qualified, etc. So you can put your diary away now. I suggest you put all this on Google docs where it will be kept forever, and you can download and print copies anytime and anywhere. You can also quickly spawn a copy to modify for a specific position. Now, let's look at the rest.

Interest and hobbies:

List your interests and hobbies that you are passionate about. Describe in greater detail, up to 40 words, where your talent has been recognised or awarded. Again, be mindful that it's not just what you did, but how you did it that will impress a prospective employer. Consider describing the interchange of life/work skills.

Awards and membership of professional bodies:
Don't hide your talents; if, for example, you got 100% in your cycling proficiency or top grade on the piano, list your achievements. Again, detail the awarding body, the date, and the grade, and describe what the award represents.

References:

Use the name, job title, and contact details of a course leader, mentor, or professor at your university, or an employer.

Contact details:

List your email, mobile number, and home address (if relevant) at the bottom of every CV page and be mindful of the differences between work and play. Don't use a silly email, such as bestlooker@email.com, as this could be seen as immature or foolish. Also, consider what you publish online. Employers check social media, even for senior roles, so expect to be Googled.

CV essentials - what is really needed

Rule number one of CVs is to think about how your CV is likely to be read. If it is going to be a small business, the personal touch with a photograph may be appreciated. If this small business is a graphic design company and you want a graphic designer's job, then clever layouts and colours will probably be appreciated. If, on the other hand, professional services firms, like accountants, would likely see this as not serious for an accountant position. If you are sending your CV to a big company, it may be rejected before a human even looks at it. Applicant Tracking Systems (ATS) machines will do the initial scan; so, in this case, a formatted template could get your CV thrown out. If your CV is likely to be read by an ATS machine, then bland (no formatting) is the best document to send. Your base CV, thus, must be as simple as possible. Not even PDF format, you need to use .doc or plain text .txt. To be sure, do not use résumé templates. These often use formatting tricks that are invisible to the eye, but are very real to the ATS. Google Docs can generate 7 different formats, so once again, I recommend using this system. It is free; all you have to do is register. I practice what I preach, and I am doing this document in Google Docs!

Make sure your CV contains these elements:

A loaded front end
Research actually shows that, on average, an initial CV scan gets only 6 seconds. So if you're opening 3 or 4 lines, don't cut it, your CV will be binned.

Keywords
Use keywords not just in the opening key skills section, but also throughout the document. Keywords at the top will probably carry more search weight, but search systems will pick up on industry specific vocabulary and words that are used in the job description

it is trying to match you for.

Measurable results
Giving measurements to what you've done adds size and scope to your achievements and invariably makes your résumé stronger and more memorable. Try to clarify your particular role in your accomplishments for previous employers and use this to build your authority.

Readability and Space
Make sure your document is well organised and easy to read. Use space to help keep your document uncluttered. Don't just read it; is it easy on the eye? You can test this by getting someone you don't know too well to read it and then explain it back to you. If the message is well understood, then you have succeeded.

Functional CVs
I have talked about the chronological ordering on work history; however, you don't have to do it this way. If you are freelancing, you could use a functional CV, but do not use this type of CV for a normal job.

CV resources on the Internet
You should not use templates for your CV when aimed at large companies. But if you feel it's appropriate, here are resources that can give you inspiration:

http://www.freesumes.com/creative-resume-templates/
https://www.livecareer.com/
http://www.fancy-resumes.com

Here is a basic template example without formatting other than bold, italic, and font size. If you subsequently want to add a photo, that is up to you. Also, if you want to make a 'fancy CV,' then you have everything for that too.

[Your Name]   *Objective: [employer's job title]* *

Summary: *[It can be called Profile or About me - two or three sentences that summarize why you qualify for the job - what you are going to do for them - must be able to read in under 10 seconds]*

Key Skills: *[List your Key skills as keywords and include industry jargon - ATS will like this]*

Employment History: *[or Education: if you prefer, particularly if you have just left school]*
Start and finish dates: *[Start and finish dates, including month and year]*
Employer's name and contact information: *[see earlier examples]*
Job title: *[Job title]*
Summary: *[brief explanation of responsibilities]*
Achievements:
- [Bullet your achievements: achievements consist of two parts - results and actions you took]
- [Quantify with numbers as much as possible: money, time amounts - proof]

Reason for leaving: *[optional, but best included - be ready for interview questions they will always ask]*

Relevant Experience:

[Optional - but can be used to explain Employment history gaps for periods of study or voluntary work]

Education:
[Qualifications in order of the most recent first; Qualification title, Location of study, Grades, Date achieved]

Interest and hobbies:
[Up to 40 words - what you did and how you did it]

Awards and membership of professional bodies:
[Optional - detail the awarding body, date, and grade, and describe what the award represents]

Any other titles you want to add:
[Languages spoken, etc.]

References:
[Name, Job title, and Contact details of the previous employer and one other - course leader, mentor, or professor at your university, or a professional person who knows you - get their agreement first]

Contact details:
[At the bottom of every (both) CV; Email, Telephone, Address]

*Some people say that you should not put an 'objective' because you can get pigeonholed, rather you should identify your goals in the cover letter so they can be tailored to each position you apply for. Despite the convenience and speed of e-mailing a résumé, cover letters are still very much required. A well-written cover letter will tell your prospective employer that you are serious about their job.

-------- *No more than two pages* ------

3. Set up and review your social media

Create and build a social media strategy

Eliminate negative content (Facebook, LinkedIn, others that you use):
Google search yourself to find any negative content that needs to be removed. Talk to your friends on Facebook and alike to get those drunken pictures deleted and do what you can to create a decent image online. Adding new positive posts can help keep negative content suppressed. If there is content that is not in your control, you need to contact the sites in question. Try this link to get some more tips: Reputation management (7)

Take social media seriously

The following stats were sourced from www.careerbuilder.com and relate to surveys done:

Social media is a double-edged sword. You can damage your reputation very easily, but you can also use social media to enhance your prospects. 41% of employers say they are less likely to interview someone with no available information online.

Don't be surprised if potential employers send you a friend request or follow your account. 36% who check social media say they do so and have indicated about 7/10 candidates accept.

About half of hiring managers say they have chosen not to hire based on what they have found online. Some examples are: provocative or inappropriate photographs, videos or information, evidence of drug taking or excessive drinking, discriminatory comments related to race, religion, and gender, negative comments about previous employers or work colleagues, and bad communication skills.

About 1/3 employers say they have hired people based on what they have found online, including: projection of a positive professional image, information supporting claimed qualifications, personality being a good fit for the company culture, showing a wide range of interests and good communication skills.

As you can see, the negative elements are very clear and need no other explanation. Let's now consider the positives. Evidently, well managed social media can equally contribute to you obtaining a position. LinkedIn is a social media that is very focused on the workplace. I suggest that you make a profile here and start to build a following. Give yourself a professional image and encourage your contacts to validate your qualifications and skills that you have listed. They are not just looking at your image; they are looking at your communication skills too (your writing skills and how you interact with your interlocutors). Your potential employer may ask to be friends on Facebook. If this is the case, then they will be able to see how you communicate with your network and see photos and videos going back many years.

Size matters; employers will be impressed if you have a large following, especially if you want to work in sales or marketing. You need to give all this some thought. Social media management is not something that happens overnight. You need a long-term strategy. What started as a giggle is now very serious. Treat social media with respect.

Check out some tips here: [10 Ways Social Media Can Help You Land a Job](#) (8)

4. General interview preparation

When you go for an interview, your prospective employers will expect you to be ready. They will, at some stage, ask you questions about your CV. As humans, they will want to get to know you, and they will want to feel that they can trust you. As employers, they will want to know you can do the job and fit in. Interviews are the opportunities brought about by your job search, so it is important to be ready. If you are following this course, the theory is that you have not started your job search yet, so to go with your basic CV, here are some basic questions you will more than likely be asked, together with suggestions about how to answer them. Before you go to a real interview, you will be busy researching the company and getting ready to respond to questions about the specific role. Figuring out answers to the basic questions at this stage will save you time later and allow the answers to sink into your subconscious, ready for when they are needed.

How to Answer the 10 Most Important Interview Questions

Don't learn your answers; just spend some time thinking how you might respond to them. Keep in mind that you need to convey the following:

1. *You will be fantastic at this new job*
2. *You are a perfect fit for this job*
3. *You really want this job*
4. *You were indispensable in your previous positions*
5. *You are likely to stay in the job if you get accepted*

The last two are a kind of paradox that poses the question, 'If you were/are so good in your last/current role, why are you in this interview?' This means that you need to be able to explain your reasons for leaving or intention to leave in a way that doesn't spook your interviewer into thinking you are flighty or incompetent and are just covering it up. You also need to be able to explain any gaps between jobs.

1. How did you find out about this position?

This question is often used as an ice-breaker to relax the candidate before going into the main part of the interview. First impressions count, so don't mess up this simple question. Before you go to any job interview, make sure that you know where you found the job. (You are supposed to be enthusiastic about this job, so you won't have forgotten!)

When you are doing your job search, keep a spreadsheet with information about the jobs you are applying for. Titles for the columns are up to you, but make sure that one of them is the source of information, i.e. the name of the website or location of the advert where you first saw the job.

If you have been referred by a friend or someone who works at the company, that should normally be a good thing. Tell them who sent you and why you were interested. That goes for the ads too. Why were you attracted to this position?

2. Can you tell me a little about yourself?

(...and how will that benefit me and my company?)

There is a little formula that you can use for this:
- Start by telling them very briefly about your family situation. (You don't have to tell them this, but it could be to your advantage. E.g. I am married with 2 children. I currently work as...)
- Next, tell them what you currently do. (About your current position, what you have achieved.)

- Then, what you have done in the past. (Your previous jobs and achievements.)
- What you want to do in the future. (Why you want to move on from your current position to a job with them and how your skills and achievements will benefit them.)
- You can mention hobbies or sporting interests, especially if they are relevant to the job you are applying for.

Remember, the objective is to tell them that you are a good fit for the job.

3. What do you know about the company?

When an employer asks this question, they want to know firstly if you have bothered to find out anything about their company. If you have, that is good, but they also want to know if you understand the company's mission and if you are enthusiastic about it. So, hunt for this information and give it some thought. It is also a good idea to know the names of the important players in the company and how they have arrived at their position. Read the about page on their website, but also search the wider Internet to find additional information.

4. Why do you want this job?

Employers want people who are enthusiastic about the position and are likely to stay in that position for some time. You can use a formula for this question.
- Firstly, express your enthusiasm for the company by showing your knowledge of the company and about their mission.
- Next, align your skills and talents with the requirements of the job. Show them that your abilities fit the role you are being interviewed for.

- People rarely have the same job for life these days. We all have a general direction of travel and personal aims. For example, as a computer programmer, I want to do roles that make me better at my job and thus, more valuable to people who want to hire me. Step three of the formula is to show them that their job fits you. That is to say, what you are doing will add to your abilities. Imply that this is what will also hold you in this role and that you won't be off looking for another job in a couple of months.

5. Why should we hire you?

(In other words, why should I hire you over everyone else?)

This question is scary, but if you are ready, then it is the best question they can ask you! This is an invitation to blow your trumpet big time! There are 4 points you need to make:

- You can do the job
- You will deliver fantastic results
- You will be a nice fit in their team and corporate culture
- One or more reasons why you are better than the rest of the candidates

There are three approaches to answering this question:

Win Win

With this approach, you present your employer with your benefits, your skills, talents, etc. Then you tell them what's in it for you, in other words, the benefits you will get from them. This will indicate to them that you will probably stay motivated and stick around for a while.

Hit the ground running

You are the expert who knows the business inside out, you already know about them (do your research). You have already told them about your skills, so put more emphasis on the idea that you won't be needing much instruction. If they hire you, you will be able to go right to work with the minimum of fuss.

The fixer

To be the fixer, you have to understand what immediate problems your prospective employer is facing. You need to show that you understand the issues and you are the person who will deliver the solution.

6. What are your greatest professional strengths?

What are your true strengths? You should think about this long before you go to an interview! Every successful person will tell you immediately what their strengths are because this brings the power of focus. If you are not sure, try asking yourself, 'What do I want to be known for?' and really work on it.

When asked this question, be truthful and honest. Talk about your strengths that are most relevant first. Understand your own skills so you can be very specific. Make sure you tell them how your strengths will benefit them with some examples.

7. What do you consider to be your weaknesses?

By asking this question, employers are trying to find out if there is something about you that is really incompatible with the work that needs to be done in the role. If you are going for a driving job, then being a self-confessed bad driver or nervous driver will make you lose the job. Beyond that, they are looking for your honesty and that you can self-reflect and have been making an effort to improve yourself. You should always focus on your strengths, but your weaker areas require work too. The amount of work you have done to improve your weakness should become the main part of your answer. A good tip is to talk about your weakness in the past tense and emphasise the work you have done and your on-going effort.

8. What is your greatest professional achievement or challenging job you have done?

Remember, at the beginning of this document, one of the 5 elements you need to convey is that 'you were indispensable in your previous positions.' This is your chance to not only tell your interviewer what you have done, but it is also your chance to provide proof of your claim.

There is little that says 'hire me' more than a track record of superb results in previous positions, but like I said before, provide evidence. Here is a little formula you can use for each achievement you want to talk about that is relevant to the job for which you are being interviewed:

Situation: Where, when, and with whom, i.e. the circumstances.
'When I was working at J. Bloggs Ltd as a contractor, 2 years ago...'

Task: What task was asked of you?
'... I was asked to 'computerise' the customer support department.'

Action: What you did.
'... so I installed an open source database, MySQL, and a ticketing system. I also wrote the help manual in HTML so it could be accessed from the company's intranet.'

Result: 'My boss was very pleased because, apart from my time, the system was set up without cost to the department's budget. The system is still fully functional today and provides customer support for the company's customer base of about 50,000 people.'

Your proof: 'My boss, Mr Bloggs, is on my list of referees, you are welcome to speak to him about this when you contact him for a reference.'

Remember the mnemonic, S-T-A-R-Y.

9. Tell me about a conflict you've faced at work, and how you dealt with it.

This question/request for information falls into the behavioural category. How did you respond to something, somebody, or some event? Essentially, they want to know if your behaviour could become an issue in the role you are applying for. These questions can be 'positive' like, 'Tell me about a time when your boss congratulated you for the good work.' There can also be 'negative' requests for information such as, 'Tell me about a time you had to deal with a conflict with one of your colleagues,' or 'Tell me about a time you made a serious error.' Your interviewer wants to know how you handle conflict and failure. They are also looking to see if you are one of 'those' people who are always at the centre of frequent disputes. By the way, if you are one of 'those' people, then make sure you go for jobs where being good at conflict is appreciated. Perhaps credit control.

To answer this type of question, you need to tell a story. So, have a think about occasions you can use to respond to this type of question in advance of interviews. Start by preparing the 'ground,' then tell your story and finish with a 'positive spin.' You might say something like this, 'Sadly, occasional conflicts are inevitable. One can be completely innocent of any wrongdoing, yet a conflict can arise from a simple misunderstanding. I can remember one such occasion when...' After you have got to the end of your 'misunderstanding' story, finish with something positive. '... For me, the first thing I do is try to understand the other person's point of view, then try to clarify any misunderstandings and, if possible, think things over before I act. Afterwards, I always try to reflect on what happened so I can be better prepared should something similar occur again.' In some cases, depending on the job you are applying for, a management role, perhaps, it may be positive to show that you intentionally initiated action where employees had been slacking. The point is, work out what stores you are going to use in advance.

10. Why are you leaving your current job?

You will always be asked this question, so be ready. Never say anything bad about your last employer. Be positive, tell them your motivation is about finding a position that fits you and your skill set better. Perhaps, even think about something that is more incidental, for example, your current job may be a long commute every day, and you want to reduce the time spent travelling. A good reason for a change that doesn't reflect badly on you in any way. If you were made redundant, just say so; it happens all the time. If you were fired, you need to think long and hard about that. Probably the best thing to do is to be honest and say so, but tell them and show if you can that you have learnt from the experience and that has made you stronger for it.

5. Write your pitch

The final part is to prepare a 'pitch' that you can use in a variety of situations when you quickly need to summarise what you do or what you want to do. One day, you may well get into some situation where you meet someone who can give you a good job. I hear you saying 'Yeah, yeah' but it happens! Indeed, it happened to me one day; on a train. I had sent a couple of résumés to a company that I wanted to work for, but had not got past the HR department. Some months later, on a train, I found myself talking to the IT director of this company. During our conversation, he asked me what I did, so I explained that I worked as a software developer and then he said I should send my résumé for his attention as they were currently looking for people with my skill set. On this occasion, I politely declined as I had already secured work and was happy with my position. However, it was both a golden and unexpected opportunity, had I been looking for a job. In any case, it is useful to prepare a pitch that can be used in both unexpected situations and as a quick-fire response to interview questions. A pitch really comes in handy at job fairs too!

'Your pitch' is a concise, compelling introduction that can be communicated in a short amount of time and may well accompany your personal 'business/job hunter card.'

Start by taking a blank sheet of paper and write down the 10 most important things you want to say about yourself, including exactly what kind of work you want to do, your top skills/abilities, what you have already achieved in your previous roles that relate to the job you want to do, what your goals are, and what makes you stand out from others. Do this as a brainstorm. If you go over 10, that's ok because part two is to consolidate and narrow your list down by optimising your statements. For example, change statements like 'I'm good at selling things' into 'I always make sure I hit my sales target;' highlight your achievements. Now, on another sheet of paper, group your statements under the following headings:

1. Who I Am
2. What I Do
3. How I Do It
4. Why I Do It
5. Who I Do It For

On another sheet, write your opening line, something that grabs attention. Then in a logical but importance first sequence, add the statements from the second sheet and blend them into your pitch.

Rehearse your pitch. Record it if you feel you need to, and try it out on your family members and friends. Get their feedback and work your pitch until you are happy with it. It may be a pain, but you will be ready to give quick-fire answers to a whole range of questions that appear in job interviews or while you are out looking for work.

You know the situation when you meet someone new, whether it is a wedding party or at a conference, they always ask, '.... and what do you do?' Next time, you will be ready to respond, not just with a simple statement like, 'I am in management' or 'I am between jobs,' but something along the lines of, 'I help people in my firm to communicate efficiently and reach their potential by ...' or 'I am searching for a new health care position to help elderly people with my nursing skills ...' Not only is it a positive mind set, but some forethought into what you say will much more naturally lead you into a conversation.

6. Prepare stationary

If you are going to send your CV in the regular post, give some thought to the paper weight and colour/tones that you may want to use to print your CV. The ideal paper density of a CV should be between 100 gsm and 120 gsm. This will give it slightly more weight and make it stand out above the rest of the CVs. Be careful, anything with a higher density than 120 gsm will make your CV feel like a thick card. Similarly, when posting CVs, make use of high-quality envelopes.

Colour: you can further improve the presentation of your CV by printing it on a cream or light cream paper as compared to the usual white sheet of paper. This has proven to be a quite effective CV marketing technique.

Keep in mind

As I mentioned earlier, think about the company you are sending your CV to. Big companies will just scan hard copies into the system, and they actually prefer to have a digital copy. The savvy job hunter will call them up and ask what they need if there is doubt. Your CV should be both digital and printable.

A job searcher card

Consider having a few cards printed with your picture and contact details as a minimum. You may want to add a brief statement about the kind of work you are looking for. You can then include this card when you send a CV or call on people. This is one way to present a picture of yourself without having to add it to your CV. If you physically call on people, your picture will help them remember you.

Organising your job search

1. **Reality check**

Not everyone is searching for their dream job. Many people are happy to take what comes, providing the job is well enough paid, and they are treated well. If this is you, then you can use a 'get a job fast' strategy as mentioned earlier. In a nutshell, this is where you draft a flexible CV with your skills and then get it out to as many employers as possible until someone sees a position for you and says 'yes' (See part 1 'prospecting CV') or you can be more choosy.

This section is for those who want to be more selective, but much also applies to the 'find a job fast' category too. It is really a case of how much customisation you want to put into each application. Tailoring your application may make the difference, but on the other hand, it makes no difference whatsoever, and your carefully drafted cover letter and CV may just get contemptuously tossed in the bin with the other 2000 rejected applications. In practice, a combination of the two approaches is probably the best bet. Ultimately, it is for you to decide.

You will read a lot of information about job searching and how you should bend over backwards in preparing each application. In theory, it's true, and reality though has made me more cynical. Employers are very happy to allow you to waste your time. Many will say, 'No, we don't accept CVs, you must fill out our application form.' 'Yeah, the same one we sent to 1000 other people for the same job,' is what they don't tell you! All because they want a few details you don't normally put on your CV like a social security number, for example. In my view, there should be a law against this! Companies should screen peoples' CVs and send application forms to those who have a chance. Most companies now don't even acknowledge that they got your CV. Pretty offensive if you put a lot of care into tailoring your CV and your cover letter. On the other hand, if you are spamming your CV, this lack of politeness is very useful because it greatly reduces the task of going through all the 'Thank you, but no' letters to find the one that says 'Please come to an interview!'

In summary

This is what I think; employers seek care and attention in applications to work for them and don't care about how much time you waste if you are unsuccessful. If you are working with a recruitment consultant who has already talked to the company about you and you have then been asked to submit a tailored CV* then, yes, put in the effort, do the full cover letter and include your CV. If you think your application will get a fleeting glance, send them your CV leaving out the cover letter, but include your job searcher card and rely on your well written and structured base CV to do its job. If you are what they are looking for, they will get in touch. Send it and get on with the next.

Very often, when working with recruitment agencies, you will have sent them your base CV, or they will have found an older CV during their searches and contact you to see if you are still available. If so, they then talk to the company to see if you sound like a fit, then if the answer is a potential 'yes,' they call you back and ask you to update your CV and tailor it for the position. If you have got this far, you actually have perhaps a 1 in 5 chance of getting hired, so it is worth spending time on tailoring your CV.

2. Job search strategies:

Keep this in mind: '45% of HR professionals find candidates on job boards (Recruitment sites), followed by their company website (18%), and employee referrals (17%). 71% said that referral candidates get high priority when deciding whom to hire.' (Source: millennialbranding.com job search study 2014 (9))

Recruitment sites

Generally, work very well. Upload your CV, and mostly, recruitment consultants will find you. Recruitment consultants fall into one of two categories. 99% are unhelpful and are just out to fill a given position and get their commission. They call you up enthusiastically, wanting you to redo your entire CV, which you do and you never hear from them again. The other 1% are exceptionally good and will take your CV and hunt for a job for you until they find one. They are extremely rare and are not usually around for long as they get promoted and disappear into management. From my own experience, my best jobs have come from recruitment sites and good recruitment consultants who have picked my CV up from searches.

Door knocking and networking

I used this method to great effect when working in sales. Call into businesses and introduce yourself. Leave your job searcher card clipped to your CV. People will hire you based on your personality and your qualifications. Here, you have a chance to project your personality from the outset. Not recommended for big companies unless you know someone, but works a treat for small businesses, such as shops, restaurants, etc. To get your foot in the door of larger firms, you need to network. Do you have any family or friends who work somewhere that interests you? If so, talk to them to see if they can get you an introduction. This, of course, is networking. If you can't find anyone you know who works at the company, track someone down on LinkedIn or Facebook. Do a search for the company name and see what comes back. Find someone and figure out a way to get to know them. Sending a friend request is probably all that's needed to open a dialogue. Networking is said to be the best way to find work. It also opens doors to unadvertised positions.

Mail drop (by regular post)

Get a list of about 500 to 1000 local companies and send them a generic letter with your prospecting CV and job searcher card by 'snail mail.' Your prospecting CV should have your introductory profile at the top so the generic letter might just appeal to the letter opener to help you by passing your CV to someone of significance in their hiring or HR department.

Try your town hall; they may be able to give you a list of sticky labels. You will have to spend an evening putting your CV and job searcher card into envelopes and sticking on stamps. Send them in the post, and you should be looking at a couple of interviews by the following week. You could use this strategy if you are a medical worker, by getting a list of hospitals or doctors' surgeries, and do the same. Make sure you are well prepared because it will cost a fair amount, so you want to be sure of a good return. Be creative about how you select your list. The town hall list is pure spam, going to many different kinds of businesses, i.e. a very broad specification: You are asking, 'Give me anything where you think I will fit in.' The hospital list is focused spam: You are asking, 'I have specific industry skills, give me a roll where you think I will fit in.'

Visit Company and Organization Web Sites and apply directly

You could do a mass email drop if you take the time to build your list. You can send up to 500 emails in a day using Gmail or other services, but email spam is not appreciated, so I don't know what results you would get as I have not tried mass emailing for jobs. I don't think it is a good idea. I think your best strategy here is to find positions that interest you on websites that interest you. Personalise a cover email and attach your basic or tailored CV. Also, create a spreadsheet that tracks your activity.

Contact / join professional organisations

Many professional organisations have field-specific job listings on their websites or in their circulars. Join if you can and start participating in meetings and other events so you can get to know people in your area of interest, particularly good for IT people. For example, Perl Mongers is an organisation for Perl programmers. Lots and lots of opportunities to meet like-minded people and best of all companies know about these groups and actively recruit from within. Aside from job searching, you will find these groups that will keep your professional knowledge up to date, and you get all sorts of inspiration.

Participate in Job Fairs

Job fairs are hosted at various locations throughout the year. Make sure you use them. Dress appropriately, ask intelligent questions, and talk about what you can do for them. Have your pitch ready together with your job seeker cards and copies of your base CV. It is also a good idea to have a pen and notebook to take quick notes after talking to people. That way, you don't get mixed up after conversations with several different firms. An old salesman's trick is to note some tiny personal details, and these can really impress. If a guy tells you that he is worried about his missing cat or his wife has just had minor surgery, the next time you talk, maybe a few weeks later, and you say, '...by the way, did 'Tiddles' get back home safely' or '...how's your wife (Mary) after the operation?'

People are really blown away that you remembered. Try it and see. (Don't tell them you made notes or you will spoil the magic!)

After the event, make sure you follow up on any promises made and take the time to send thank you letters/emails to any companies that seem interesting.

Temping/agency work

Another way to get your foot in the door is to do temping work. You may even discover that you like working in this manner. When I was driving trucks, I preferred doing agency work to having a full-time job and did so for a number of years. I liked going to work in different places, and I liked the option of being able to take days off when I wanted to. Best of all, a lot of temping assignments on your résumé won't damage your prospects.

A quick search on Google for 'temp work agencies + your city' will find what you need to get started. Don't be afraid to be choosy, both with the agencies and the jobs. Ask the agencies what companies they have as customers so that you can take jobs that exercise your skills and only work in companies that interest you and can offer you full-time work when you demonstrate how good you are.

It usually takes a week or two to get set up with an agency, and you can get set up with more than one. A word of caution though, agencies are in competition with each other and are often chasing the same customers. If they see you working for one of their customers via another agency, it is all too easy to get embroiled in an unwelcome inter-agency rivalry and offend both agencies; resulting in no work. Stay strictly neutral.

3. Admin and spreadsheets

Now that you have started applying for jobs and sending out your CV, you will very quickly realise that you want to track your activity if for no other reason than to avoid sending duplicate applications. Here is a link to a free template, courtesy of Google docs:

https://drive.google.com/previewtemplate?id=0AkZyK4st_9NpdGY1ZHhTMnVnVVQyT0F6b0daR1BYUEE&mode=public&ddrp=1# (10)

Once loaded, you can export a .xlsx version that will work with Microsoft Excel or LibreOffice if you prefer.

4. Cover letters

Cover letters are both a blessing and a curse. If done correctly, they let you thoroughly explain how your experiences will make you a perfect fit for a specific position. Let your enthusiasm show how you will directly benefit the company, not what you will gain from them. In a nutshell, your cover letter needs to convey these 3 points. Keep them in mind while following the rules:

1. You're going to perform extremely well in this job.
2. You're a very likable person.
3. You're really going to fit in.

The rules:

A. Write a cover letter that's specific to the job and the company you're applying to, explaining why you're interested in that particular position.
B. Find someone in the organisation to write to. Address the letter personally to them. 'Dear Mr Bloggs.'
C. Keep your cover letter to a single page.
D. Pay attention to details - spelling and grammar.
E. Write in a style that is neither too formal nor informal - friendly, be yourself.
F. Before you start writing, look at the job description and identify what skills are being asked for and their priority of importance.
G. Tell them how your experience will fit with the required skills and how that will benefit them from day one.
H. Talk about your strengths and then how your strengths will benefit them (never talk about your weaknesses).
I. Don't list, tell a story - consider using an anecdote (this will add to your 'likableness' and individuality).
J. Tell them why you are interested in their company/organisation and why you think you will fit into

      their culture.
- K. Do not regurgitate your résumé - expand on achievements listed on your résumé. Include leadership positions, relevant awards, and advanced skill sets right from the beginning.
- L. As with your résumé, use numbers and statistics to show them that you've made your mark in your past positions. Employers love to see the numbers.

When you finish your letter, proofread it very carefully. I also suggest you give it to someone else to check too.

Landing the job (closing the deal)

1. Dress for success

First impressions are formed within the first 30 seconds of meeting you, like it or not; your appearance is the first thing people notice and plays a major role in a decision to hire you as the interviewers try to visualize you in the position they are trying to fill. Your attire is making an unspoken statement about yourself. For men, make sure you are clean and well-groomed. Unless told differently, wearing a suit is normal, so you won't lose points for that, but make sure it is clean, pressed, and fits well; shoes polished. Show your individuality with your tie, but think about the job you are being fitted for.

I am certainly not going to tell women how to dress! However, the general advice is to wear your 'power outfit,' but at the same time, you must feel comfortable in it. Here is an article from those in the know: http://www.wikihow.com/Dress-for-Success-as-a-Woman (11)

If I am interviewing, I expect to see people who have at least made an effort. After all, if your appearance doesn't say, 'I am ready to give this job my best shot,' you are going to really hamper your chances during an interview.

2. Specific interview preparation - research

Here are some things you should learn about an employer before going for an interview:

What skills and experience are they looking for?

I have told you to do this several times already, and here it is again. Look at the job description and remind yourself about what they require. Look also for the priorities they give relating to the skills that they are asking for.

Their culture, mission, and values

Read the company's website and try to get a feel of what they are about. What are the company values? Try to get a feel for culture by reading between the lines. Very often, a company will state their mission; find it and give it some thought. Ask yourself if their aim aligns with your values? As a candidate, you must be able to say that you are a good fit for the company during your interview. In fact, a Millennial Branding study (9) says 'Following a national survey (USA) of job seekers and HR professionals, 43% of the 2,978 respondents said that 'cultural fit' was the single most important determining factor when making a new hire.' You can also learn more about the company culture by following the organisation on its social media networks.

News and recent events about the employer

The firm's recent activity will preoccupy the thoughts of your interviewers, and they will often talk about what's happening in the firm's near future and what the company is doing or trying to achieve, especially if they want the successful candidate (you!) to be part of it. You will probably be able to glean this information from their website. Very often, because it can be about a specialised application of their products, this information can come over as somewhat esoteric. You may, therefore, feel somewhat confused. This is a good thing because you now have a base in which to ask some intelligent questions.

Who are the key players in the organisation?

These individuals can be managers, directors, and especially the CEO/president of the company. Find out who they are by reading the website 'About' page. Google them and see what makes them tick. Often, you will be asked 'What do you know about the company/us?' Make sure you know the boss' name at least.

Clients, products, and services

The focus of the company's website will be about their products and services. Very often, they will also give case studies about the work done with important clients as examples. As a potential employee, you need to know about the type of work you will be doing if you get the job. Feast on this information, it will serve you well in the interview.

Look outside of the company website

Google the company and see what other sites say. This information can be revealing. On the company's website, you will see their 'propaganda' other sites could be revealing. If negative things have been stated, you may be looking at some of the company's current issues. Understand them, what can you do to help?

The person interviewing you

If you can find out about who will be interviewing you, then that can be an advantage. 'Praemonitus praemunitus' or forewarned is forearmed!

3. Second interviews

What's the difference between a first and second interview?

For most employers who extend the hiring process into more than one meeting, the first interview is about scooping off the cream. They are looking for people who are qualified and who will fit in. The second or subsequent interviews are naturally more competitive, so the questions are likely to be more intense, and you will probably be introduced to people who, if hired, you will be working with. The burning question for them is why you? What can you offer that is special and puts you above the other applicants? Are your skills really as good as you claim? Will you have issues getting to work, which could affect your performance? Additionally, they will also want to take into consideration the opinions of their current employees who will have to work with you. The focus is now on the details that separate you from the other candidates. Here are some examples of questions that come up during second interviews:

Are there any reasons why you wouldn't want this job?

If you have any reservations, this is a good time to get them clarified. They may well be asking this because you are looking like a very good option for them and they want to be sure to get you on board. Perhaps, questions about salary or training. Hopefully, something they can address. Start by saying something positive about the firm or the job. Then pose your questions. Perhaps something like this:

'During my visits here, I have come to realise there is a fabulous working atmosphere and all members of your staff are friendly and helpful, and that's something I find really appealing. My only reservation is the salary. It is a little lower than I expected. Will my salary be increased at the end of my probation period? How does it work?'

What are the main attributes you think are needed for this role?
You know the answer to this because they told you on the job description! Respond by talking about the essential skills listed in the job description. Remember S-T-A-R-Y?
Use this as a base, thinking on your feet you may respond to something along the lines of:

'I think 'insert the job description essential skills' are the most important skills necessary for this role. When I was 'situation' I demonstrated these skills when I was asked to do 'insert task,' I was able to achieve 'insert accomplishments' resulting in 'insert results and your proof (figures if possible).'

What would you change about the company?

You have been given the opportunity to show off how well you have researched the company. Hopefully, something will have occurred to you during the research process, so have it prepared for the interview. It is important to say why you've said it and what benefits such a change would bring.
What are your career goals? Where do you see yourself five years from now?
What the interviewer really wants to know is that you've thought about your future and if you are likely to stick around. Be passionate about the company and the industry, and talk about your desire to develop your career within their organisation. Don't give the impression that you will be leaving sometime soon for whatever reason.

What salary are you looking for?

If it's not been covered already, this question may arise. My advice is to do your research. Find out what the job is worth in the region and ask for a range that covers it. For example, if you find out that the average salary is £47k, then ask for between £45 and £50k - I use GBP because I am a Brit, but you get the idea. Use a search engine to find an average salary checker that covers your location. Here is one that I have used before:

https://www.totaljobs.com/salary-checker/salary-calculator (12)

4. Thank you notes/letters

If you have got this far in the interview process, this is the moment to close it down with your last final effort. Put your computer aside and write a handwritten thank you note. By all means, draft the note with a computer to help check your spelling and to adjust the text till you are happy with the content and layout. But at the end, get your fountain pen out, and in your best handwriting, on quality stationery, write an old fashioned thank you letter.

Before you start, ask yourself these questions:
1. Did the interviewer(s) enjoy the conversation?
2. In which parts of the interview did you really connect with them?
3. What kind of interviewing style did they have (warm and friendly or strictly business)?

Make sure you cover these 3 important points:
1. Thank the person for meeting with you and use their name when addressing them
2. Mention something you liked about the interview
3. Repeat your interest in the job and give a brief recap of your skills

Do not to be casual with your language or tone; your letter is relatively informal, but don't use informalities, emoticons, or text speak such as 'LOL.'

Customise your thank you letter, and proofread it for grammar and spelling mistakes. A poorly drafted letter at this stage can ruin all the good impressions you made during your interviews. You can send a letter to each of the interviewers, but to me, that is starting to look a bit staged. Personally, I would include a line in my letter to the 'chief' interviewer, asking them to convey your thanks to the others who were involved - but it's up to you, every situation is different.

Here are some links to sample letters that I have seen that you could use for inspiration:

https://www.monster.com/career-advice/article/sample-interview-thank-you-letter (13)

http://www.jobinterviewtools.com/blog/sample-thank-you-letter-after-interview/ (14)

5. First day on the job

Get yourself well prepared in advance, make sure your clothes are ready, and you get a good night's sleep. Prepare and ask questions about how you can best succeed in your new job and try to demonstrate your curiosity and desire to learn, but don't go over the top with too many questions. Your first days are about listening, observing, and generally getting the feel of how the place works. Project high energy and enthusiasm. It goes without saying to be punctual. Showing up 15 minutes early, dressed ready to play your part is a good start. Set your mobile to silent mode.

Don't be shy, talk to your new peers, and get to know them. You may well be invited out to lunch. This is a great way to get to know people and is probably the reason why you are being asked. Be ready to accept. Show interest in both your peers and your new job. Use and learn people's names and be yourself, be relaxed, and don't forget to smile.

Read your job description or any literature on what your responsibilities are. You may also have unstated tasks you need to be aware of, figure them out. Try to really understand what the most important aspects of your job that will bring you success in the eyes of your employers are. What you think is successful conduct and what they think can be two different things. Make sure you understand their priorities and understand what they want from you. After that, you can add your priorities to make your mark on the position.

Be aware of office politics and 'cliques,' especially negative cliques and negative people. As time goes by, you will start to identify these people and groups, keep your distance from them and try, rather, to associate with people and groups who have a positive attitude. Finally, study the decision-making process. How are decisions made in the company and where does the authority lie?

Shortened links mentioned in the text

Page 17

1) Test: what are your strengths?	https://goo.gl/PvaMky
2) Personality test	https://goo.gl/uTSuZw
3) Test to help you find your values	https://goo.gl/OzDOkP
4) INTJ	https://goo.gl/ovhMnA
5) INTP	https://goo.gl/vTqK2l

Page 18

6) The Holland Code Career test	https://goo.gl/Y9Qbjf

Page 30

7) Reputation management	https://goo.gl/iYUh8l

Page 31

8) 10 Ways Social Media Can Help You Land a Job	https://goo.gl/EGDCbK

Page 42 and 48

9) millennialbranding.com job search study 2014	https://goo.gl/Eap4Gy

79

Page 45

| 10) Spreadsheet template | https://goo.gl/zSclkN |

Page 47

| 11) Dress for success for women | https://goo.gl/6hqkga |

Page 51

| 12) Salary calculator | https://goo.gl/aOLfzi |

Page 52

| 13) monster.com sample thank you letter | https://goo.gl/lHTqG9 |
| 14) jobinterviewtools.com sample thank you letter | https://goo.gl/WLnrYO |

Other reading

Wikihow
http://www.wikihow.com/Be-Successful-in-Life
http://www.wikihow.com/Dress-for-Success-as-a-Woman
http://www.wikihow.com/Excel-in-Life
http://www.wikihow.com/Perform-Self-Hypnosis
http://www.wikihow.com/Avoid-Exercises-That-Age-You-Faster

Ted talks
The most important lesson from 83,000 brain scans (https://goo.gl/lxHHTG)
Get into the right frame of mind for an interview (https://goo.gl/cXSRcj)

Getting personal help – Skype consultation

I hope you find this book useful and I hope, as a result of my advice and your efforts, you land yourself a really good job! I will have to tell you that my objective is to work for myself these days. I love to write software, and I am currently working on a little project of my own. I like to work over the Internet and interact with people, so I still do my English lessons for students who want to learn English and other projects such as this. That is why I want to offer you help by personalised direct consultation on Skype. If you would like me to check your CV or give you a live practice interview, please check my website for more details:

Skype consultation offer (https://goo.gl/7rCR2k)

www.ingramcontent.com/pod-product-compliance
Lightning Source LLC
Chambersburg PA
CBHW070110210526
45170CB00013B/811